Date: 12/30/11

**J 599.674 DOU
Doudna, Kelly,
It's a baby African elephant! /**

SandCastle™

Baby
African Animals

It's a Baby

African Elephant!

Kelly Doudna

Consulting Editor, Diane Craig, M.A./Reading Specialist

ABDO
Publishing Company

Published by ABDO Publishing Company, 8000 West 78th Street, Edina, Minnesota 55439.

Copyright © 2009 by Abdo Consulting Group, Inc. International copyrights reserved in all countries.

No part of this book may be reproduced in any form without written permission from the publisher. SandCastle™ is a trademark and logo of ABDO Publishing Company.

Printed in the United States.

Editor: Liz Salzmann
Content Developer: Nancy Tuminelly
Cover and Interior Design and Production: Mighty Media
Photo Credits: Digital Vision, Peter Arnold Inc. (C. & M. Denis-Huot, J.P. Ferrero & J.M. Labat, Jochen Tack), ShutterStock

Library of Congress Cataloging-in-Publication Data

Doudna, Kelly, 1963-
   It's a baby African elephant! / Kelly Doudna.
      p. cm. -- (Baby African animals)
   ISBN 978-1-60453-149-7
   1. African elephant--Infancy--Juvenile literature. I. Title.

QL737.P98D666 2009
599.67'4139--dc22
                           2008005466

SandCastle™ Level: Fluent

SandCastle™ books are created by a team of professional educators, reading specialists, and content developers around five essential components—phonemic awareness, phonics, vocabulary, text comprehension, and fluency—to assist young readers as they develop reading skills and strategies and increase their general knowledge. All books are written, reviewed, and leveled for guided reading, early reading intervention, and Accelerated Reader® programs for use in shared, guided, and independent reading and writing activities to support a balanced approach to literacy instruction. The SandCastle™ series has four levels that correspond to early literacy development. The levels are provided to help teachers and parents select appropriate books for young readers.

Emerging Readers	Beginning Readers	Transitional Readers	Fluent Readers
(no flags)	(1 flag)	(2 flags)	(3 flags)

SandCastle™ would like to hear from you. Please send us your comments and suggestions.
sandcastle@abdopublishing.com

Vital Statistics

for the African Elephant

BABY NAME
calf

NUMBER IN LITTER
1

WEIGHT AT BIRTH
220 pounds

AGE OF INDEPENDENCE
11 years

ADULT WEIGHT
8,000 to 14,000 pounds

LIFE EXPECTANCY
60 to 70 years

Elephant calves can walk an hour or two after they are born.

An elephant's pregnancy lasts 22 months, the longest of any mammal.

Elephants live in herds.
A herd is made up of cows
and their offspring.

Mother elephants are
called cows.

When a calf is born, other elephants in the herd touch it with their trunks.

The oldest cow guides the herd. She knows the best places to find food and water.

Elephant calves have shorter trunks than adults. Calves nurse with their mouths. Calves stop nursing when their tusks begin to grow.

Elephants are herbivores. They eat mostly grass, fruit, leaves, and bark.

Elephants greet each other by twisting their trunks together. They also touch each other's faces with their trunks.

An elephant's trunk is both its upper lip and its nose.

Lions and hyenas prey on elephant calves. They are easier to catch than adult elephants.

The adults surround the calves when predators are near. This makes it very hard for them to hurt the calves.

Young female elephants remain with their birth herd. Young males leave the herd and form their own small groups.

Fun Fact

About the African Elephant

Adult elephants have molars
the size of bricks!

Glossary

expectancy – an expected or likely amount.

herbivore – an animal that eats mainly plants.

herd – a group of animals that are all one kind.

independence – no longer needing others to care for or support you.

molar – a back tooth with a flat surface for grinding.

nurse – to feed a baby milk from the breast.

offspring – the baby or babies of an animal.

predator – an animal that hunts others.

pregnancy – the period of time that a female mammal carries her developing offspring inside her body.

prey – to hunt or catch an animal for food.

To see a complete list of SandCastle™ books and other nonfiction titles from ABDO Publishing Company, visit **www.abdopublishing.com**.

8000 West 78th Street, Edina, MN 55439

800-800-1312 • 952-831-1632 fax